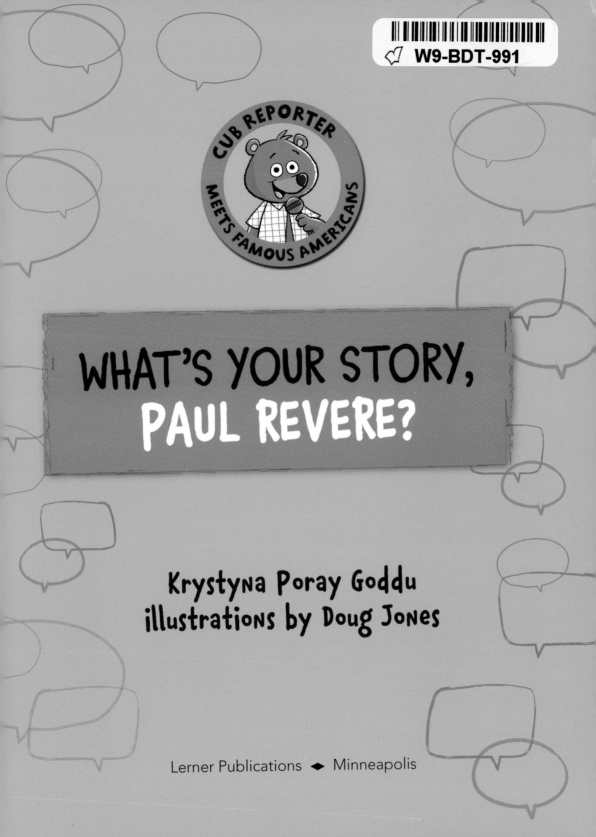

CUB REPORTER MEETS FAMOUS AMERICANS

WHAT'S YOUR STORY, PAUL REVERE?

Krystyna Poray Goddu
illustrations by Doug Jones

Lerner Publications ◆ Minneapolis

Note to readers, parents, and educators:
This book includes an interview of a famous American. While the words this person speaks are not his actual words, all the information in the book is true and has been carefully researched.

Lerner Publications Company
A division of Lerner Publishing Group, Inc.
241 First Avenue North
Minneapolis, MN 55401 USA

For reading levels and more information, look up this title at www.lernerbooks.com.

Main body text set in Avenir LT Pro 45 Book 15/21. Typeface provided by Linotype AG.

Library of Congress Cataloging-in-Publication Data

Goddu, Krystyna Poray.
    What's your story, Paul Revere? / Krystyna Poray Goddu.
      pages cm — (Cub reporter meets famous Americans)
    Includes index.
    ISBN 978-1-4677-8781-9 (lb : alk. paper) — ISBN 978-1-4677-9641-5 (pb : alk. paper) — ISBN 978-1-4677-9642-2 (eb pdf)
    1. Revere, Paul, 1735–1818—Juvenile literature. 2. Statesmen—Massachusetts—Biography—Juvenile literature. 3. Massachusetts—Biography—Juvenile literature. 4. Massachusetts—History—Revolution, 1775–1783—Juvenile literature. I. Title.
F69.R43G63 2016
973.3'311092—dc23 [B]   2015013553

Manufactured in the United States of America
1 – VP – 12/31/15

Table of Contents

Hi, friends! Today I'm talking to Paul Revere, a very important person from history. Paul, why are you important? Can you tell us about yourself?

Paul says: Of course! I was one of the **patriots** who helped early Americans stand up to the British. In the 1700s, the United States wasn't a free country. It was a group of **colonies**. The colonies were ruled by Great Britain. We colonists had to follow Great Britain's laws. But we didn't always agree with those laws. So we found ways to fight back. I became a secret messenger to help the cause. I also went on a midnight ride that helped the colonists become free.

Paul Revere helped the American colonies break free from Great Britain. This painting of Paul was created in the early 1800s.

Where and when were you born?

Paul says: I was born in 1734 in Boston, Massachusetts. My father was a **silversmith**. He made objects out of silver. When I was twelve, I became a silversmith too. My father taught me how to cut and pound silver. We made bowls, tea sets, and many other things. When I wasn't with my father, I spent time playing and swimming with my friends. My father died in 1754. I had to support my family. I learned to draw and print pictures that I could sell to make more money.

Paul grew up in Boston, Massachusetts. This illustration shows what the city looked like in the 1770s.

Paul made this silver teapot in 1765.

When did you become a secret messenger?

Paul says: I became a secret messenger after some of the colonists started to **protest**, or speak out against, British laws. First, I started a secret group with some friends. Great Britain had sent soldiers to keep an eye on the colonists. Our group spied on those soldiers and told other patriots what they were doing. By about 1773, I had started carrying messages for the group. I'd done some messenger work before, but this was different. I had to work in secret because I was carrying detailed notes about the soldiers. To make sure the messages got to everyone quickly, I traveled on horseback. I was a very fast horseback rider!

In the 1770s, some colonists wanted to protest British laws. They held secret meetings to talk about their plans. Paul helped carry their messages across the colonies.

How did colonists feel about having British soldiers in Boston?

Paul says: We colonists hated having British soldiers in town. The soldiers didn't like us much either. Some colonists made fun of the soldiers' uniforms. Kids called the soldiers lobsters because they wore red coats. Soldiers and colonists were always getting into fights. And in March of 1770, things got even worse. There was a *huge* fight between colonists and British soldiers. Five colonists lost their lives in this **conflict**. It became known as the Boston Massacre.

This illustration shows British soldiers fighting a crowd of colonists. Colonists and British soldiers didn't get along.

What happened after the Boston Massacre?

Paul says: The colonists were furious that five people had died. The soldiers who killed the colonists had to go to court. A judge listened to what had happened during the conflict. I wanted the judge to find the soldiers **guilty**, so I created a picture of the conflict. The picture showed the soldiers standing by the victims' bodies.

The judge did not believe my picture. He found the soldiers innocent. So then I made another picture. This picture showed the soldiers actually shooting the colonists. I knew that when the colonists saw it, they would get even angrier. I hoped that when they got angrier, they would fight harder against the British. And they did!

Paul created this picture of British soldiers shooting at colonists during the Boston Massacre in March 1770.

What did the colonists do to fight the British?

Paul says: They began to protest more. One huge protest had to do with a **tax** the British government put on tea. Taxes help pay for the government. But we had no say in how the colonies were run. So we didn't think it was fair to pay a tax to the British. One night in 1773, a group of colonists crept onto three ships that were docked in Boston Harbor. The ships were carrying British tea. The colonists dumped all the tea into the harbor! This protest came to be called the Boston Tea Party. This was our way of letting the British know they couldn't tell us what to do anymore.

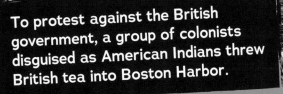

To protest against the British government, a group of colonists disguised as American Indians threw British tea into Boston Harbor.

What happened after the Boston Tea Party?

Paul says: The protest made the soldiers very angry. They decided to go to Lexington, Massachusetts, to arrest two important patriot leaders there. My group got word of the plan ahead of time. They asked me to ride my horse to Lexington to warn people. So I worked out a plan with the **sexton** at a Boston church. We agreed he'd hang one light in the church tower if the soldiers were coming by land. He'd hang two lights if they were coming by sea. If I didn't make it to Lexington, the lights would tell people along the way how the soldiers would arrive. The sexton hung two lights. Then I took off on my famous ride!

A VIEW OF PART OF THE TOWN OF BOSTON IN NEW ENGLAND AND BRITTISH SHIPS OF WAR

Paul created this picture showing the British arriving in Massachusetts by sea.

Was your
ride dangerous?

Paul says: My ride was very dangerous. British soldiers were watching all the roads because they wanted to keep people from leaving Boston. If I got caught trying to go to Lexington, I could be arrested. That's why I left for my ride late at night. If I left in the dark, British soldiers wouldn't be able to see me as easily. That meant I had a better chance of not getting caught. The timing of my journey is why it came to be called my midnight ride.

Paul rode on horseback to warn people of the British soldiers' attack. He was known as a fast rider.

Did you make it to Lexington without getting caught?

Paul says: I did, but I had a very close call. Soon after I left for Lexington, I saw two soldiers hiding behind a tree. They saw me too. I quickly turned my horse around. The soldiers came after me, but I was too fast for them! I galloped away and didn't slow down until I got to Lexington. Then I rode my horse up to all the houses there and warned the patriots that the British soldiers were on their way.

This illustration shows Paul warning the people of Lexington during his midnight ride.

Was your mission complete after you rode to Lexington?

Paul says: Not quite. I'd also hoped to ride to Concord. I'd gotten word that the British soldiers planned to destroy patriots' **ammunition** supplies there. I wanted to warn the patriots. So I started out for Concord. But things didn't go smoothly on the way to Concord. The soldiers saw me again. This time, they captured me! Lucky for me, the soldiers thought they heard a fight breaking out between other soldiers and some patriots. They wanted to help the soldiers, so they left me behind. I never made it to Concord. But I did escape the British. I had to walk back to nearby Lexington because the soldiers had taken my horse. In the meantime, two of my fellow patriots were able to take over my mission.

Paul was able to spread the news of the British soldiers' arrival to many people before he was captured.

What happened between the British soldiers and the colonists after your ride?

Paul says: When I got to Lexington, one of the very first things I heard was gunshots. It turned out that the shots were the start of a war. It was the American Revolutionary War (1775–1783). This war went on for eight long years. Many people lost their lives. But it was the beginning of something that I'd been hoping for. It meant that the colonists were fighting for their freedom from the British soldiers.

The first battle of the Revolutionary War is known as the Battle of Lexington and Concord.

How did the war turn out?

Paul says: The colonists won! This meant we didn't have to listen to the British soldiers anymore. We were free to make our own laws. In 1776, we officially formed our own country—the United States of America. And by 1789, we'd elected our country's first president, George Washington. It was wonderful to have our independence from the British at last.

After the Revolutionary War ended, George Washington *(shown on horseback)* became the first US president.

How did the American colonies change because of you?

Paul says: I had long believed that colonists should have freedom from the British. I did everything I could to help make that happen. By creating my pictures, going on my midnight ride, and delivering messages, I helped American colonists come together to form a new country. If I hadn't done what I did, Americans might never have been free from British rule. I'm proud to say that I helped create the United States of America.

Timeline

1734: Paul Revere is born in Boston, Massachusetts.

1754: Paul's father dies, and Paul takes over the family silversmith business.

1757: Paul marries Sarah Orne.

1765: Paul helps to form the Sons of Liberty in Boston around this time. This secret group fought back against the British.

1770: The Boston Massacre takes place. Paul creates pictures of the massacre.

1773: The Boston Tea Party takes place. Later that year, Paul marries Rachel Walker after Sarah Orne's death.

1775: Paul rides to Lexington to warn patriots that British soldiers are on their way.

1783: The United States of America formally wins its independence from Great Britain.

1813: Rachel dies.

1818: Paul dies in Boston, Massachusetts.

Glossary

ammunition: objects such as bullets and shells that are shot from weapons

colonies: areas belonging to a country but far away from it

conflict: a serious disagreement

guilty: responsible for doing something wrong

patriots: American colonists who wanted to be free from British rule

protest: to show or express strong disagreement

sexton: a person who takes care of church buildings

silversmith: a person who makes objects out of silver

tax: money people pay to the government to use for government services

LERNER

Expand learning beyond the printed book. Download free, complementary educational resources for this book from our website, www.lerneresource.com.

SOURCE

Further Information

Books

Amstel, Marsha. *The Horse-Riding Adventure of Sybil Ludington, Revolutionary War Messenger.* Minneapolis: Graphic Universe, 2012. Learn more about what it was like to be a messenger during the Revolutionary War.

Edwards, Roberta. *Who Was Paul Revere?* New York: Grosset & Dunlap, 2011. Explore the story of Paul Revere's life and the colonial times he lived in.

Hicks, Dwayne. *Paul Revere: American Patriot.* New York: PowerKids, 2013. Learn more about Paul Revere through illustrations and maps in this biography.

Websites

Kids and History—Paul Revere, a Brief Biography
http://kidsandhistory.net/paulvm/h2_hist.html
See an illustrated timeline of the important events in Paul Revere's life.

The Paul Revere House—Articles for Kids
https://www.paulreverehouse.org/kids/articles.html
On this website, you'll find articles, activities, and other materials about Paul Revere.

Social Studies for Kids—Fun Facts
http://www.socialstudiesforkids.com/funfacts/paulrevere.htm
Visit this site to learn more about Paul Revere's famous ride.

Index

Photo Acknowledgments

The images in this book are used with the permission of:
© Massachusetts Historical Society/Bridgeman Images,
p. 5; © Boltin Picture Library/Bridgeman Images, p. 7
(bottom); Library of Congress, pp. 7 (top), 13; © North
Wind Picture Archives/Alamy, pp. 9, 19, 21; © Stock
Montage/Getty Images, p. 11; © iStockphoto.com/
duncan1890, p. 15; © Revere, Paul (1735–1818) Historic
New England, Boston, Massachusetts, USA/Bridgeman
Images, p. 17; © Classic Image/Alamy, p. 23; © National
Army Museum, London/Bridgeman Images, p. 25;
© Universal History Archive/UIG/Bridgeman Images, p. 27.

Front cover: © GL Archive/Alamy.